RIF
Reading Is
Fundamental
of Southern California

A NEW BOOK
for
MY LIBRARY

Reading Is Fundamental
of Southern California
7250 Bandini Blvd., #208
Los Angeles, CA 90040
323-890-0876
www.rifsocal.org

I Wonder Why

Records Are Broken

and Other Questions About Amazing Facts and Figures

Simon Adams

KINGFISHER

NEW YORK

KINGFISHER
LONDON & NEW YORK

Published in the United States by Kingfisher,
175 Fifth Ave., New York, NY 10010
Kingfisher is an imprint of Macmillan Children's
Books, London.

Distributed in the U.S. by Macmillan,
175 Fifth Ave., New York, NY 10010
Distributed in Canada by H.B. Fenn and Company Ltd.,
34 Nixon Road, Bolton, Ontario L7E 1W2

ISBN 978-0-7534-6291-1

Library of Congress Cataloging-in-Publication Data has
been applied for.

Kingfisher books are available for special promotions
and premiums. For details contact:
Special Markets Department, Macmillan,
175 Fifth Avenue, New York, NY 10010.

For more information, please visit
www.kingfisherpublications.com

First American Edition August 2009
Printed in Taiwan
9 8 7 6 5 4 3 2 1
1TR/0309/SHENS/PICA/126.6MA

Illustrations by Planman Technologies (India) PVT Ltd.;
cartoons by Peter Wilks.

CONTENTS

4 When does a record become
a record?

4 Why do we keep records?

5 Why are records
broken?

6 Which hurricane
blew the hardest?

6 Which records
can blow you away?

7 Why does the wind spin?

8 Where do you most need
an umbrella?

8 When do you need to wear
a hard hat?

9 How heavily can snow fall?

9 Where on Earth sizzles the most?

10 Where do angels fall?

10 How deep is the deepest
fresh water?

11 Which river is the longest?

11 When was an ice cube
like Jamaica?

12 Which mountain towers over
the world?

13 Who first climbed the highest
mountains?

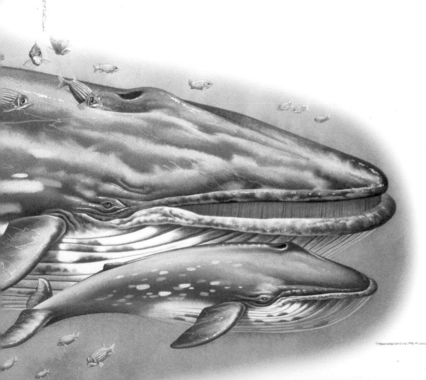

13 Are mountains getting bigger?

14 Which volcano blew its top the most?

14 What gives Earth the shakes?

15 How do waves get as tall as houses?

16 Which continent contains the most countries?

16 Just how crowded is planet Earth?

17 Which is the most crowded country?

18 How quickly can you sail around the world?

19 Which nonstop flight came first?

19 Who accidentally set a new record?

20 Have humans reached the stars?

20 How deep have humans sunk?

21 How fast can you cross a desert?

22 Can you jump like a flea?

22 How fast can two legs carry you?

23 Which is the sportiest sport?

24 Which is the world's biggest city?

24 Who are the greatest tunnelers?

25 How high can we build?

26 Which insect feeds the world?

26 How much does the biggest baby weigh?

27 Where do big birds fly?

27 Which animals are the speediest?

28 Which shark is a gentle giant?

28 How big do snakes' appetites get?

29 Which hairy spider is a Goliath?

30 Which planet is king?

31 How brightly can a star shine?

31 Can we measure a galaxy?

32 Index

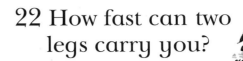

When does a record become a record?

Everything that can be measured in some way becomes a record. We can measure the length, width, height, weight, quantity, age, speed, or volume of almost everything in the human and natural world, and we keep the results as records.

● Some records are kept for a very long time. The weather has to be recorded in the same place every day for 30 years before we know what the climate is like in that location.

Why do we keep records?

● Not every record is serious. There is a record for eating baked beans quickly!

We all keep records. We keep a record of when the sun rises each day so we know when it will rise on the same day next year. We keep records to help us know what to aim for—how much higher to jump or how much faster to run. And we keep records for fun!

Why are records broken?

Records are broken because people run faster and live longer, giant tortoises get older, winds blow stronger, and temperatures rise higher and drop lower. Each time a new extreme record is achieved, an old record is broken.

● American athlete Mildred "Babe" Zaharias set three new world records in the high jump, javelin, and hurdles in 1930–1932. She also won four major golf titles and became a championship basketball player.

Which hurricane blew the hardest?

In October 2005, Hurricane Wilma blew around the Gulf of Mexico with wind speeds of up to 180 mph (295km/h). It killed a total of 23 people in the Caribbean, Mexico, and the United States.

● Hurricanes are named in alphabetical order, with a girl's name alternating with a boy's name.

Which records can blow you away?

Wind is a stream of air that moves from one place to another. The power of the wind is measured on the Beaufort scale. The scale runs from force 0 to force 12.

Force 2 is a light breeze.

Force 8 is a gale.

Force 12 is a hurricane.

Why does the wind spin?

Sometimes columns of fast-moving, spiraling air inside thunderclouds snake down to the ground. These columns suck in air at speeds of up to 250 mph (400km/h). They are known as waterspouts at sea and tornadoes on land.

● Tornadoes are only about 330 ft. (100m) wide at the base, but they can lift cars, houses, cows, and sometimes even people off the ground.

Where do you most need an umbrella?

The wettest place on Earth is Mawsynram, India. It rains an average of 467 in. (11,870mm) every year, most of it during the monsoon season. The most continuously rainy place in the world is Mount Waialeale, Hawaii, where it rains about 350 days every year.

When do you need to wear a hardhat?

● Hail is formed when water droplets freeze to form ice. The frozen lumps then fall as hail.

A hardhat might be handy in Aurora, Nebraska. The world's largest hailstone, measuring 7 in. (178mm) across, fell there on June 22, 2003. It is reported that hailstones killed 92 people in Bangladesh on April 14, 1986, and 25 people were killed in Henan province, China, on July 19, 2002.

How heavily can snow fall?

An amazing 1,244 in. (31,102mm) of snow fell on Mount Rainier in Washington from February 19, 1971, to February 18, 1972. That is about the same height as 19 people standing on one another's heads!

● The hottest places on Earth are near lightning, when the air is heated briefly to about 54,000°F (30,000°C)—five times hotter than the Sun's surface.

Where on Earth sizzles the most?

On September 13, 1922, the temperature at Al'Aziziyah in the Libyan desert reached 136°F (57.8°C). In Dallol, Ethiopia, the temperature averaged 93.9°F (34.4°C) for six years from 1960.

Where do angels fall?

Angel Falls, in Venezuela, is the world's tallest waterfall, measuring 3,212 ft. (979m). The wind blows much of the water into mist as it falls. About 4.5 million gal. (17 million L) of water per second pour over Boyoma Falls in Africa.

How deep is the deepest fresh water?

Lake Baikal in Russia is the deepest and biggest freshwater lake in the world. At its deepest, it reaches 5,371 ft. (1,637m) below the surface. It holds more than one-fifth of the world's fresh water.

Which river is the longest?

If you were to unwind the Nile River in Africa and measure its length from its source to the sea, you would discover that it is 4,132 mi. (6,650km) long. That makes it the longest river in the world, only 155 mi. (250km) longer than the Amazon River in South America.

Mediterranean Sea

Sahara Desert

Red Sea

Nile River

Lake Victoria

When was an ice cube like Jamaica?

● Only about one-tenth of an iceberg is visible above the water's surface. The rest lurks under the water.

In 2000, iceberg B-15 broke away from the Ross Ice Shelf in Antarctica. It measured 183 mi. (295km) long and 23 mi. (37km) wide, making it almost the same size as the island of Jamaica in the Caribbean. It probably weighed about 3 billion tons.

Which mountain towers over the world?

If you reach the top of Mount Everest, you are standing on the highest mountain in the world. Everest, in the Himalayas, Asia, is 29,035 ft. (8,850m) high. Thirteen of its neighbors are also more than 26,245 ft. (8,000m) high. They tower over every other mountain in the world.

● The height of Mount Everest is measured from sea level. If you measure from the seabed, the world's highest mountain is Mauna Kea in Hawaii, at 33,474 ft. (10,203m) high.

Who first climbed the highest mountains?

Italian climber Reinhold Messner was the first person to climb all 14 of the world's highest mountains above 26,245 ft. (8,000m). He climbed the first peak in 1970 and the last in 1986. In 1978, he became the first person to climb Mount Everest without bottled oxygen.

Movement of plate upward

Mountain range

Are mountains getting bigger?

Mountains can get taller. They sit on top of vast plates of rock the size of a continent. These plates float on top of the liquid interior of Earth. Sometimes they bump into one another, making one plate rise up. This causes a mountain such as Everest to rise at about 0.16 in. (4mm) a year.

Which volcano blew its top the most?

On August 27, 1883, Krakatau in Indonesia exploded with a bang that could be heard 3,000 mi. (4,800km) away. It threw rocks 34 mi. (55km) into the sky, and dust fell as far as 3,310 mi. (5,330km) away over the next ten days. More than 36,380 people were killed.

● Earthquakes send out shock waves that travel through the ground. The wave size is measured on the Richter scale. The biggest earthquake on the scale (9) is one billion times greater than the smallest (0).

What gives Earth the shakes?

An earthquake is a sudden movement on Earth's surface, often caused by a fault in the crust. The worst one occurred in Shaanxi, China, on January 23, 1556. It measured 8 on the Richter scale and killed 830,000 people.

How do waves get as tall as houses?

Earthquakes, volcanic eruptions, and landslides can cause huge waves called tsunamis to form out at sea. Tsunamis can travel up to 500 mph (800km/h). The world's deadliest struck the Indian Ocean on December 24, 2004, killing more than 225,000 people.

● Some volcanoes erupt continuously. Kilauea in Hawaii has been active since 1983, throwing out 177 cu. ft. (5m^3) of lava every second.

Which continent contains the most countries?

Africa contains more countries than any other continent – 53 of the world's 194 countries are found here. Many African countries are very new. In 1950, there were only 82 separate countries in the whole world.

● There are 43 landlocked countries in the world, with no direct link to the sea. Two – Liechtenstein in Europe and Uzbekistan in Asia – are double landlocked. Their peoples go through two other countries in order to reach the seaside.

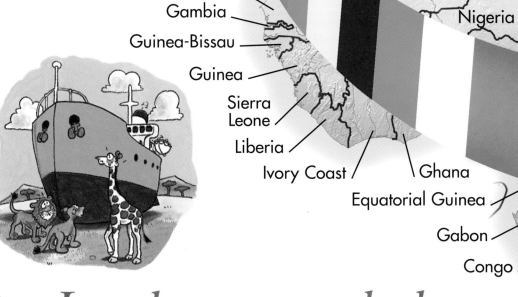

Tunisia
Morocco
Western Sahara
Algeria
Mauritania
Niger
Mali
Cameroon
Senegal
Gambia
Nigeria
Guinea-Bissau
Guinea
Sierra Leone
Liberia
Ivory Coast
Ghana
Equatorial Guinea
Gabon
Congo
Angola
Namibia

Just how crowded is planet Earth?

● The world's population is rising at roughly 2.5 people per second, 216,000 per day, and 1,512,000 per week!

In 2008, the world's population was roughly 6,724,400,000 people. That is around 45 people in every square kilometre. Six out of every ten of those people live in Asia, most of them in the big cities of China, India and Japan.

Which is the most crowded country?

Monaco in southern Europe is famous for its motor racing, but it is also the most crowded country in the world. Its 32,671 people are packed into three-fourths of a square mile. In comparison, only 4.4 people live in each square mile of Mongolia.

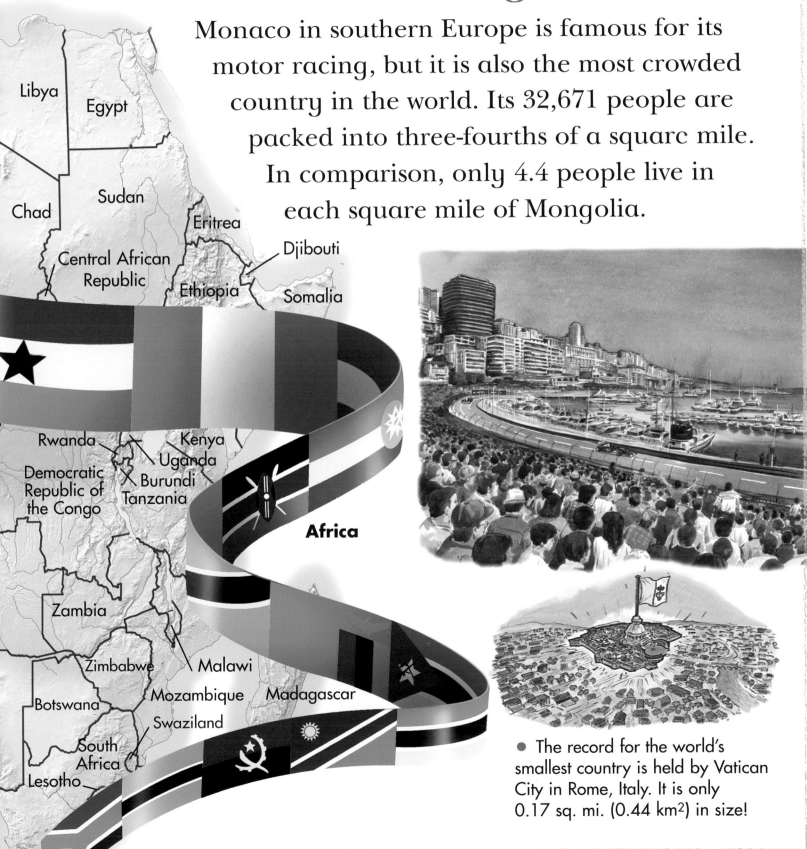

Libya

Egypt

Chad

Sudan

Eritrea

Central African Republic

Djibouti

Ethiopia

Somalia

Rwanda

Kenya

Uganda

Democratic Republic of the Congo

Burundi

Tanzania

Africa

Zambia

Zimbabwe

Malawi

Botswana

Mozambique

Madagascar

Swaziland

South Africa

Lesotho

● The record for the world's smallest country is held by Vatican City in Rome, Italy. It is only 0.17 sq. mi. (0.44 km^2) in size!

How quickly can you sail around the world?

The quickest time a boat has sailed around the world without stopping is 50 days, 16 hours, and 20 minutes. This record time was achieved in March 2005 by French sailor Bruno Peyron and his crew of 13 onboard the giant catamaran *Orange II*.

● The first person to sail single-handedly around the world without stopping was British sailor Robin Knox-Johnston in 1968–1969. It took him 313 days.

Orange II

B-29 refueling tanker

Refueling hose

Lucky Lady II

Which nonstop flight came first?

The first plane to fly nonstop around the world was the U.S. Air Force B-50 bomber *Lucky Lady II*. The journey, in March 1949, took 94 hours and 1 minute, and the plane refueled four times in midair. *Lucky Lady II* had 13 crew members onboard.

● In 1960, the U.S. Navy nuclear submarine *Triton* became the first craft to sail underwater around the world.

Who accidentally set a new record?

In 1519, Ferdinand Magellan set a new record when he sailed west from Spain across the Atlantic and Pacific oceans to the Philippines. After he died there, Juan Sebastián Elcano and 17 crew members sailed the *Victoria* home, becoming the first to sail around the world.

Have humans reached the stars?

Between 1969 and 1972, 12 American astronauts landed on the Moon and another 12 flew around the back of the Moon. No one has reached the stars. Unmanned spacecraft, however, have left the solar system and flown toward the closest stars.

● Humans can survive underwater without breathing for about nine minutes and can descend to about 655 ft. (200m). Emperor penguins can reach a depth of 870 ft. (265m), and sperm whales frequently dive to 3,940 ft. (1,200m).

How deep have humans sunk?

The deepest place on Earth is the Challenger Deep at the bottom of the Marianas Trench in the Pacific Ocean. On January 23, 1960, the bathyscaphe *Trieste* descended 35,797 ft. (10,911m) to the trench floor.

● It is not just humans that have flown in space. Cats, dogs, monkeys, frogs, spiders, worms, snails, fish, rats, mice, and other creatures have all made the journey.

How fast can you cross a desert?

● The fastest a person has ever cycled over 200m is 9.772 seconds, which is about 67 ft. (20.5m) per second.

Someone has gone at an incredible 763 mph (1,228km/h)—faster than the speed of sound! This record was set in the Black Rock Desert in Nevada by Andy Green on October 15, 1997. His jet-propelled car *Thrust SSC* flew along at 12.7 mi. (20.5km) per minute.

Can you jump like a flea?

A flea can jump 130 times its own height, but the record for an adult male human is only 8 ft. (2.45m) and an adult woman 6.9 ft. (2.09m)— both less than twice the average human height. Even using a pole, an adult man can vault only 20.1 ft. (6.14m), or three times a man's average height.

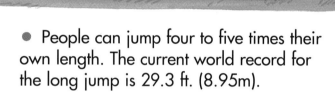

● People can jump four to five times their own length. The current world record for the long jump is 29.3 ft. (8.95m).

How fast can two legs carry you?

The fastest man on two legs over 100m is Usain Bolt, a Jamaican athlete. At the Beijing Summer Olympic Games in 2008, he ran the course in 9.69 seconds, a new world record. The record for a woman, 10.49 seconds, was set by American sprinter Florence Griffith-Joyner in 1988.

● One sport not included in the decathlon is cell-phone throwing. A world championship has been held in Finland every year since 2000.

● Women compete in the eight events of the heptathlon. It is like the decathlon, only with one less track race and no discus-throwing event.

Which is the sportiest sport?

In the decathlon, athletes compete in ten different sports over two days. On day one, they complete the 100m sprint, long jump, shot put, high jump, and a 400m run. On day two, they complete the 110m hurdles, discus, pole vault, and javelin before finishing with a 1,500m race.

Which is the world's biggest city?

Tokyo, Japan, is the biggest city in the world. About 32,450,000 people live there. Seoul, South Korea, and Mexico City, Mexico, are the next two biggest cities, with around 20,500,000 people each.

● Some suspension bridges are so long that their two towers point slightly away from each other. This is because the surface of Earth is curved.

Who are the greatest tunnelers?

At the moment, the greatest tunnel builders are the Japanese. Their 33.4-mi. (53.8km)-long Seikan railroad tunnel links Honshu and Hokkaido islands. In 2017, the Swiss Gotthard Base Tunnel under the Alps will be open. That will be an amazing 35.5 mi. (57.1km) long.

How high can we build?

The tallest inhabited building in the world is the Taipei 101 tower in Taiwan, with its 101 floors. When the Burj Dubai (Dubai Tower) in the United Arab Emirates (UAE) opens in 2009, it will dwarf every other structure in the world at 2,684 ft. (818m).

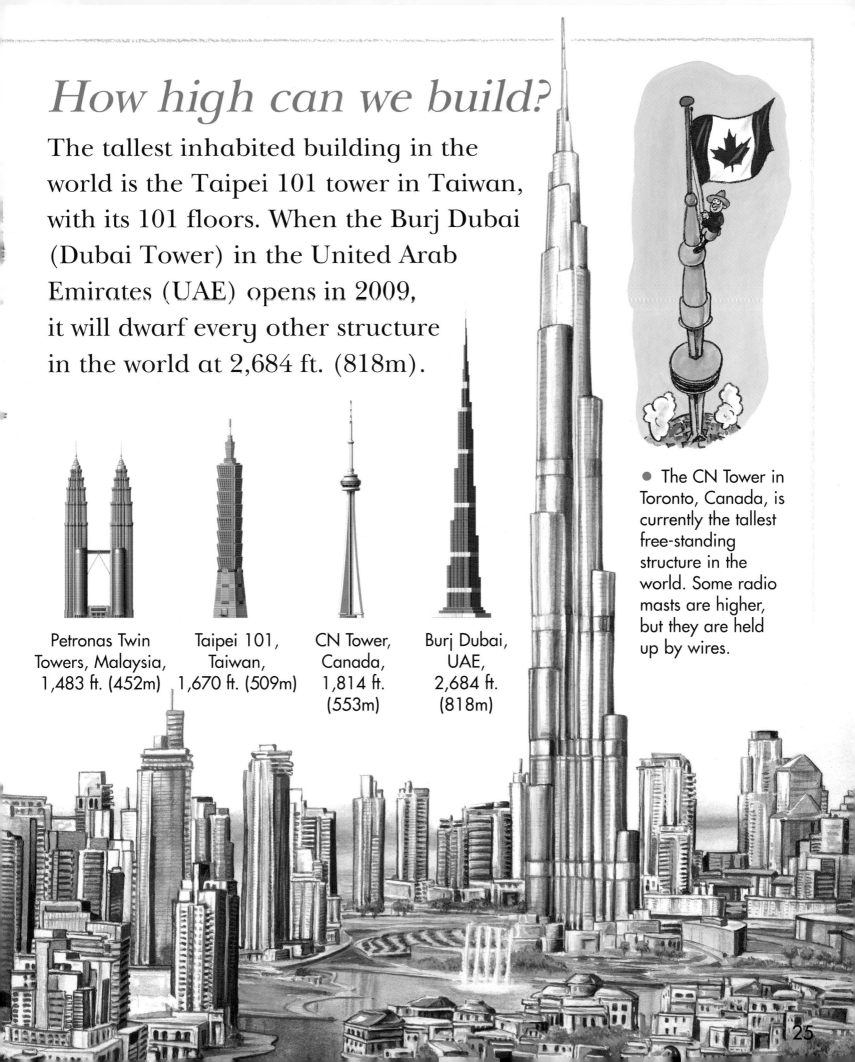

Petronas Twin Towers, Malaysia, 1,483 ft. (452m)

Taipei 101, Taiwan, 1,670 ft. (509m)

CN Tower, Canada, 1,814 ft. (553m)

Burj Dubai, UAE, 2,684 ft. (818m)

● The CN Tower in Toronto, Canada, is currently the tallest free-standing structure in the world. Some radio masts are higher, but they are held up by wires.

Which insect feeds the world?

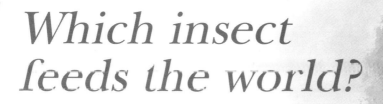

Honeybees are the only insects that provide food which humans can eat. They make honey to feed themselves in winter. Any leftovers are harvested by beekeepers. The bees visit up to five million flowers to make 1kg of honey.

● Baby blue whales grow at an amazing 90kg a day. They grow into the world's biggest creatures, weighing in at around 130 tonnes.

How much does the biggest baby weigh?

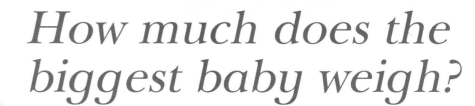

The blue whale gives birth to a 2,000kg whopper that is already 7m long. A human baby only weighs about 3.2kg at birth and is around 46–55cm long.

Where do big birds fly?

The biggest flying bird is the albatross. It lives in the Antarctic Ocean and the northern Pacific Ocean and has a wingspan of 12.1 ft. (3.7m). The largest flightless bird is the 9-ft. (2.74m)-tall ostrich, which lives in Africa.

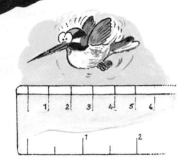

- The tiny bee hummingbird is 2.2 in. (5.7cm) long and weighs only 0.06 oz. (1.6g), about half the weight of a penny.

- The Arctic tern flies from the Arctic to the Antarctic and back every year, a round trip of 24,850 mi. (40,000km).

Which animals are the speediest?

The fastest creature is the peregrine falcon, which dives at speeds of up to 185 mph (298km/h). On land, the cheetah is the quickest, racing along at 65 mph (105km/h). Some humans can manage 23 mph (37km/h) over 100m.

Which shark is a gentle giant?

The whale shark is the biggest fish in the world. It grows up to 39 ft. (12m) long and can weigh 23 tons (21 metric tons). Yet this vast beast is harmless to humans and other fish. It eats only plankton —the tiny plants, animals, and bacteria that drift around in the ocean.

How big do snakes' appetites get?

An African rock python will easily swallow a 130 lb. (59kg) antelope. Reticulated pythons eat pigs weighing 132 lbs. (60kg) or more. And one 17-ft. (5.17m)-long python once ate a 14-year-old Malay boy.

● The coastal taipan of Australia is so deadly that its venom could kill 120 people.

Which hairy spider is a Goliath?

The goliath bird-eating spider lives in the South American rainforest. It is as big as a dinner plate, with legs up to 9.8 in. (25cm) long. It eats birds and other small creatures and is harmless to humans although it can sting.

● The banana spider of Central and South America lives hidden in bunches of bananas. It produces enough venom to kill six adults.

Giant storm known as the Great Red Spot

● Light travels at an amazing 186,280 mi. (300,000km) per second. Even at that speed, sunshine is eight minutes, 17 seconds old when we see it. Light from our closest star takes 4.22 years to reach us.

Planets only

● There used to be nine planets in our solar system, but in 2006, Pluto was downgraded to become a "dwarf planet."

Which planet is king?

Jupiter is the biggest planet in our solar system. The planet is 88,846 mi. (142,984km) wide. It is so big that it is 2.5 times the size of the other seven planets in the solar system combined. Jupiter is named after the Roman king of the gods.

How brightly can a star shine?

The brightest star we can see is the Sun because it is the closest star to us. But the brightest star we can see from Earth in the night sky is Sirius, which is also called the Dog Star. It is more than 20 times brighter than the Sun.

Can we measure a galaxy?

A galaxy is a large group of stars held together by gravity. We measure the size of a galaxy by how long light takes to travel from one side to the other. The Abell 2029 galaxy is 5.6 million light-years wide, 56 times wider than the Milky Way galaxy (above).

Index

A

Africa 10,
   11, 16, 27, 28
Antarctica 11, 27

B

bees 26
birds 27
bridges 24
buildings 25

C

cheetahs 27
cycling 21

D

deserts 9, 21
diving 20

E

earthquakes 14, 15
   Richter scale 14
   Shaanxi, China 14

H

hailstones 8
hurricanes 6
   naming of 6
   Wilma 6

I

icebergs 11

L

lightning 9

M

Marianas Trench 20
Milky Way 31
monsoons 8
Moon 20
mountains 12, 13
   Everest 12, 13
   Himalayas 12
   Mauna Kea 12

P

planes 19
planets 30
   Jupiter 30
population 16, 17
   cities 24

R

rain 8
rivers 11
   Amazon 11
   Nile 11

S

sailing 18, 19
   Orange II 18
snakes 28
snow 9
solar system 20, 30
space 20, 21
   galaxies 31
   stars 20, 31
spiders 29
sports 22–23
   athletes 5, 22
   decathlon 23
   heptathlon 23
   long jump 22
   pole vault 22
   running 22

submarines 19, 20
   Trieste 20
   Triton 19
Sun 30, 31

T

Thrust SSC 21
tornadoes 7
tsunamis 15
tunnels 24

V

Vatican City 17
volcanoes 14, 15
   Kilauea, Hawaii 15
   Krakatau 14

W

waterfalls 10
waterspouts 7
whale sharks 28
whales, blue 26
wind 6
   Beaufort scale 6

KEY TO MEASUREMENTS

U.S. Customary	Metric
°F degrees Fahrenheit	°C degrees Celsius
ft. foot	m meter
in. inch	cm centimeter
mi. mile	mm millimeter
mph miles per hour	km kilometer
oz. ounce	km/h kilometers per hour
lb. pound	
gal. gallon	g gram
	kg kilogram
	L liter